for GCSE

Practice for book H2 part A

PATHFINDER
EDITION

Contents

PUBLISHED BY THE PRESS SYNDICATE OF THE UNIVERSITY OF CAMBRIDGE
The Pitt Building, Trumpington Street, Cambridge, United Kingdom

CAMBRIDGE UNIVERSITY PRESS
The Edinburgh Building, Cambridge CB2 2RU, UK
40 West 20th Street, New York, NY 10011-4211, USA
477 Williamstown Road, Port Melbourne, VIC 3207, Australia
Ruiz de Alarcón 13, 28014 Madrid, Spain
Dock House, The Waterfront, Cape Town 8001, South Africa

http://www.cambridge.org

© The School Mathematics Project 2002
First published 2002

Printed in Italy by Rotolito Lombarda
Typeface Minion   *System* QuarkXPress®

A catalogue record for this book is available from the British Library

ISBN 0 521 01338 0   paperback

Typesetting and technical illustrations by The School Mathematics Project

1 Forming and solving equations

Section A

1 Solve each of these equations.

Check that your answer works in the original equation.

(a) $2x + 6 = 3 - x$ (b) $3x - 2 = 5 - 4x$ (c) $7 - 5x = 4x - 11$

(d) $8x + 2 = 3x - 8$ (e) $3x - 5 = 7 + 9x$ (f) $7x + 5 = 7 + 3x$

2 Solve each of these equations

(a) $3x - 5 = 3 - 9x$ (b) $3 - 2x = 9 + 10x$ (c) $4 - 5x = 3x + 20$

(d) $8x - 9 = 6 + 2x$ (e) $5 - 23x = 11 - 5x$ (f) $1.5 - 9x = 5 - 2x$

3 Solve each of these equations

(a) $9 - \frac{1}{2}x = 15 + x$ (b) $\frac{1}{8}x - 12 = 13 - \frac{1}{2}x$ (c) $\frac{5}{6}x - 5 = \frac{1}{2}x - 6$

(d) $3 - \frac{x}{14} = 9 - \frac{x}{2}$ (e) $\frac{2}{15}x + 19 = 7 - \frac{2}{3}x$ (f) $1 - \frac{x}{4} = 7 - \frac{x}{2}$

Section B

1 Solve each of these equations

(a) $2(x + 3) = 10$ (b) $9(x - 1) = 36$ (c) $12(x + 3) = {}^-12$ (d) $5(3x - 2) = 35$

2 Solve

(a) $3(x + 3) = 15 + x$ (b) $2(x - 6) = 5x - 6$ (c) $3(4x - 1) = 2(1 + x)$

(d) $2(5x + 6) = 3(2x + 5)$ (e) $2(x + 2) = x - 4$ (f) $2(5x - 1) = 7(x + 4)$

3 Solve

(a) $\frac{x - 3}{4} = 1$ (b) $\frac{3x + 2}{5} = 4$ (c) $\frac{5x - 3}{7} = 6$

(d) $\frac{8 - 2x}{5} = 3$ (e) $\frac{9x + 1}{2} = 14$ (f) $\frac{20 - 4x}{3} = 7$

4 Solve

(a) $5(3 - x) + 7(x - 2) = 9$ (b) $3(2x - 1) + 5(3x + 2) = 49$

(c) $3(4x - 1) - 2(3x + 2) = 17$ (d) $8(2x + 1) + 4(x + 4) = 16$

(e) $4(2x + 3) - 5(3x + 2) = 9$

5 Solve

(a) $\frac{3x + 1}{2} = 2x - 3$ (b) $\frac{5x - 2}{3} = 3x - 10$

(c) $\frac{6 - 2x}{4} = 19 + 3x$ (d) $2(3x + 3) + 5(2x + 5) = 63$

(e) $4(3x + 1) - 3(5 - 4x) = 1$ (f) $6(4x - 3) - 3(5 - 2x) = 57$

Section C

1 Solve each of these equations

(a) $\frac{3x+3}{4} = \frac{5x-6}{3}$

(b) $\frac{6x-2}{3} = \frac{8x+2}{5}$

(c) $\frac{4x+3}{5} = \frac{5x+2}{6}$

(d) $\frac{1}{2}(6x-3) = \frac{1}{5}(8x+3)$

2 Solve

(a) $\frac{5x-3}{2} - \frac{2x+1}{3} = 11$

(b) $\frac{6x+1}{2} - \frac{4x+1}{3} = 2x$

(c) $\frac{3x+2}{4} - 3(x-5) = \frac{x}{3}$

(d) $8 - \frac{x}{5} = 2(x-7)$

Section D

1 Find the size of each angle in these shapes.

(a)

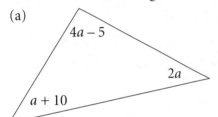

(b)

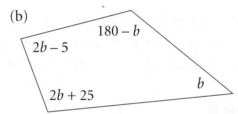

(c)

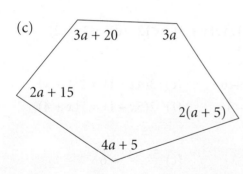

(d)

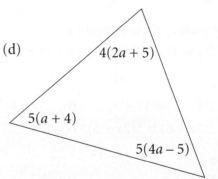

2 The perimeter of each of these shapes is 120 cm.
   Find the length of each side.

(a)

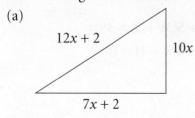

(b)

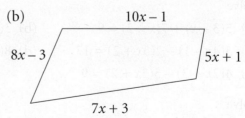

(c)

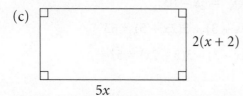

3 Work out the starting number in each of these 'think of a number' puzzles.

(a) I think of a number.
   I subtract 8 and multiply by 6.

   My answer is double the number I first thought of.

(b) I think of a number.
   I subtract 2 then multiply by 4 and take off 1.

   My answer is 3 times the number I first thought of.

(c) Jack and Alex both think of the same number.
   Jack subtracts 8 and then multiplies the result by 5.

   Alex halves his number and then adds 14.
   They both end up with the same number.

(d) Narinder and Brian both think of the same number.

   Narinder subtracts 5 from her number and divides the result by 7.
   Brian divides his number by 2 and then subtracts 10.

   They both end up with the same number.

2 Accuracy

Section B

1 What are the upper and lower bounds of all the numbers for which:
   (a) 6.4 is the nearest tenth
   (b) 0.1 is the nearest tenth
   (c) 50 is the nearest whole number
   (d) 250 is the nearest ten
   (e) 4.09 is the nearest hundredth

2 Write down the upper and lower bounds for each of these.
   (a) The length of a room is 2.8 m, correct to 2 significant figures.
   (b) The weight of a baby is 4.20 kg, correct to 3 significant figures.
   (c) The volume of a pond is 3.1 m³, correct to 2 significant figures.
   (d) The length of a work surface is 1370 mm, correct to the nearest millimetre.
   (e) The capacity of a jug is 350 ml, correct to the nearest 10 ml.
   (f) The weight of a parcel, to the nearest 100 g, is 1.5 kg.

Section C

1 Find the upper and lower bounds of the total weight of three boxes each weighing 5.7 kg to the nearest 0.1 kg.

2 The dimensions of a room are measured as 3.7 m and 2.1 m, correct to 2 significant figures.
   Find the upper and lower bounds of
   (a) the perimeter of the room and
   (b) the area of the room.

3 Lara records the distances she cycles each day for a week. On five days she cycles 35 km and on two days she cycles 16 km. The distances are measured to the nearest kilometre.
   Find the upper and lower bounds of the distance she cycled during the week.

4 The dimensions of this trapezium are given to the nearest centimetre.

   Calculate the maximum possible area of the trapezium.

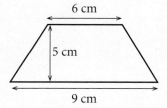

6

Section D

1 A piece of wood is 1.6 m long, correct to the nearest 10 cm.
   Jack cuts off a piece 72 cm long, correct to the nearest centimetre.

   Find the upper and lower bounds of the length of wood remaining.

2 A partially empty tank has a total capacity of 2500 litres, to the nearest 10 litres.
   To fill the tank, 1245 litres of oil, measured to the nearest litre, needs to be added.

   Find the upper and lower bounds of the original quantity of oil in the tank.

3 In this right-angled triangle side $a = 4.7$ cm
   and side $c = 5.4$ cm, both to the nearest
   0.1 cm.

   Calculate the upper and lower bounds
   for the side b.

   Give each answer to 4 significant figures.

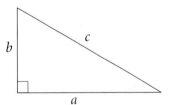

Section E

1 The power of an electrical circuit is given by the formula
   $$P = \frac{V^2}{R}$$

   where P is the power in watts, V is the voltage and R is the resistance in ohms.

   Calculate the upper and lower bounds of the power if the voltage is 240 volts and the
   resistance is 410 ohms, both measured to 2 significant figures.

2 A bottle of medicine contains 100 ml, correct to the nearest millilitre.
   One dose of medicine is 5 ml.

   If the doses are measured correct to the nearest millilitre, what is the minimum number
   of doses in the bottle?

3 The population of England in 2000 was 50.0×10^6, correct to 3 significant figures.
   The area of England is 130 000 km², correct to 3 significant figures.

   Calculate the upper and lower bounds for the population density (people per km²) of
   England in 2000.

   Give your answers correct to 4 significant figures.

3 Scaling

Sections A and B

1 This shape is to be enlarged with scale factor 2.5.
Make a sketch of the enlargement showing its dimensions.

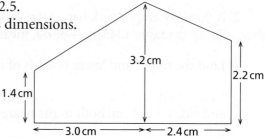

2 Shape P is enlarged with scale factor 2 to give shape Q.
Shape Q is enlarged with scale factor 3 to give shape R.

What is the scale factor of the enlargement

(a) from shape P to shape R

(b) from shape Q to shape P

(c) from shape R to shape Q

(d) from shape R to shape P

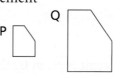

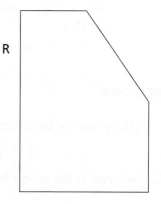

3 The scale factor of an enlargement from a shape A to a shape B is 1.4.
The scale factor of an enlargement from B to a shape C is 1.25.
(a) What is the scale factor of the enlargement from A to C?

(b) What is the scale factor of the scaling from C to B?

4 A drawing is scaled down on a photocopier set at 70%.
The copy is then scaled down on a setting of 60%.
What is the scale factor from the original drawing to the final copy?

5 A standard photographic colour print is 150 mm by 100 mm.
Neil uses his scanner and computer to produce
an enlargement 390 mm by 260 mm.

(a) What is the scale factor for the enlargement?

(b) What is the area factor?

6 This semicircle has an area of 12 cm².
Work out (i) the scale factor and (ii) the area of the enlarged shape
when the semicircle is enlarged with scale factor

(a) 5   (b) 2.2   (c) $\frac{5}{3}$ (d) 0.8

7 What scale factor corresponds to each of these area factors?

  (a) 4   (b) 1.69   (c) $2\frac{1}{4}$ (d) 8

8 An architect draws a building to a scale of 1 : 50.
A door is drawn 42 mm high and 18 mm wide.
How big **in metres** will the door be in real life?

9 Two mirrors are the same shape.
The area of glass in the larger one is double that in the smaller.
The width of the larger mirror is 30 cm.
What is the width of the smaller mirror?

10 A plan of a room is drawn to a scale of 1 : 20 .
A large rug in the room has an area of 7 m².
What area in cm² will this be represented by on the plan?

11 A road contractor is working from a plan on a scale of 1 : 500.
A stretch of road to be re-surfaced covers 32.5 cm² on the plan.
What is this area in m² on the real road?

Section C

1 Sphere B has twice the diameter of sphere A.

  (a) What is the area factor from the surface of A to the surface of B?

  (b) What is the volume factor from A to B?

2 Cuboids V and W are similar.
The scale factor from V to W is 1.1 .

  (a) What is the volume factor from V to W?

  (b) Given that the volume of V is 2000 cm²,
  what is the volume of W?

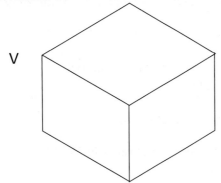
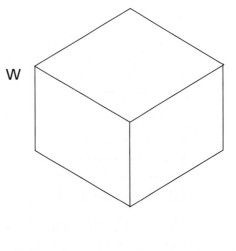

3 Find the volume factor for a scaling whose scale factor is

  (a) 3   (b) 6   (c) 15   (d) 0.9   (e) 0.2

4 These two glasses are similar-shaped.
The smaller glass holds 108 cm^3 of liquid.
What does the larger one hold?

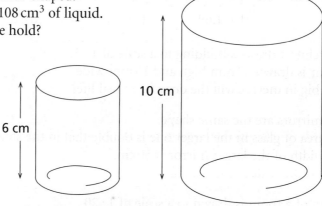

6 cm

10 cm

5 Find the scale factor of an enlargement whose volume factor is

(a) 125   (b) 729   (c) 216 000   (d) 27 000   (e) 0.064

6 These two bread tins are the same shape.
One is designed for a 1 pound loaf,
the other for a 2 pound loaf.
What is the scale factor from the
smaller one to the larger one?

2 pound loaf

1 pound loaf

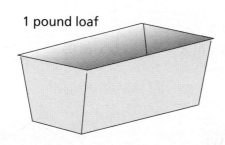

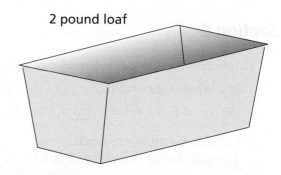

7 Two tubes of toothpaste are the same shape but different sizes.
The large tube holds 350 g of toothpaste. The small tube holds 200 g.
The small tube is 12.0 cm long.
How long is the large tube?

8 F and G are similar objects, made from the same material.
F's surface area is 6.25 times that of G.
The mass of G is 100 g.
Find the mass of F.

9 Three similar objects have surface areas in the ratio $4 : 25 : 49$.
Give the ratio of their volumes.

10 A model for a sculpture is made on a scale of $1 : 20$.
The model has a volume of 8000 cm^3.
What will the volume of the finished sculpture be, in m^3?

Mixed questions 1

1 The diagram shows the dimensions of a trapezium.
   The perimeter of the trapezium is 32 cm.

   Find the area of the trapezium.

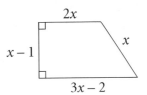

2 Vinod has a picture that measures 8 cm by 10 cm.
   He enlarges it so that it its area is twice as big.

   What are the new dimensions of the picture?

3 Solve these equations.

   (a) $\dfrac{p-7}{3} = \dfrac{3p}{2}$

   (b) $\dfrac{y+2}{3} - \dfrac{y+5}{5} = 1$

4 Draw a triangle PQR with PQ = 5 cm, QR = 8 cm and RP = 10 cm.
   Shade the locus of points in the triangle that are closer to PQ than to QR and are closer to Q than P.

5 (a) Copy and complete the table of values for $y = 2x^2 - 3x$ for $^-2 \le x \le 3$.

x	$^-2$	$^-1$	0	1	2	3
y			0			9

   (b) On a sheet of 2 mm graph paper plot the graph of $y = 2x^2 - 3x$ for $^-2 \le x \le 3$.

   (c) Use your graph to solve the equation $2x^2 - 3x = 5$.

   (d) What happens if you try to solve the equation $2x^2 - 3x = ^-2$?
       What can you say about the equation $2x^2 - 3x = ^-2$?

6 A box of chocolates contains 8 milk chocolates and 4 dark chocolates.
   Alex takes two chocolates from the box at random.

   Use a tree diagram to find the probability that he takes

   (a) two dark chocolates

   (b) one milk and one dark chocolate

7 (a) Write down the 10th term of the sequence which begins 1, 7, 13, 19, ...

   (b) Write down an expression for the nth term of the sequence.

   (c) Is 473 a term of the sequence? Explain your answer.

   (d) Calculate the number of terms in the sequence 1, 7, 13, 19, ..., 355.

8 The surface of a drive is to be a 10 cm layer of tarmac, measured to the nearest 1 cm.
   The drive has been measured as 9 m long and 3.6 m wide, both to the nearest 10 cm.

   Calculate the maximum possible volume of tarmac required for the drive.

9 Q is directly proportional to $\sqrt{P}$.
When $P = 25$, $Q = 30$.

  (a) Find the equation connecting Q and P.

  (b) Find   (i)   the value of Q when $P = 9$ (ii)   the value of P when $Q = 60$.

10 Karen makes candles in the shape of square-based pyramids.
These two candles are similar.

  (a) The volume of the smaller candle
is $96\,\text{cm}^3$.

    What is the volume of the larger
candle?

  (b) Karen makes another similar candle
that has a volume of $12\,\text{cm}^3$.

    What is the height of this candle?

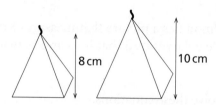

11 This table shows the age and gender distribution of the employees in a company.

Age	16–21	21–30	30–45	45–65
Males	28	35	47	42
Females	19	41	38	30

Mary is carrying out a survey about employee satisfaction in the company.
She wants to take a stratified sample of 50 employees from the whole company.

Calculate how many in the sample should be

(a) males aged 16–21

(b) females aged 30–45

(c) aged 45–65

12 (a) Copy the grid and triangle ABC.

  (b) Rotate triangle ABC 90° clockwise about (1,1).
Label this triangle A′B′C″.

  (c) Rotate triangle A′B′C′ 90° anticlockwise
about (0,⁻1).
Label this triangle A″B″C″.

  (d) Describe fully the single transformation
which maps triangle ABC onto triangle A″B″C″.

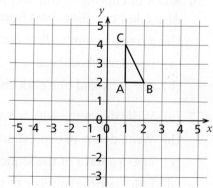

4 Solving quadratic equations

Section A

1 Solve the following by factorising

(a) $x^2 - 8x + 15 = 0$

(b) $x^2 + 10x + 21 = 0$

(c) $x^2 - 8x + 12 = 0$

(d) $x^2 - 3x - 10 = 0$

(e) $x^2 + 5x - 24 = 0$

(f) $x^2 - 7x = 0$

2 Solve these equations by rearranging and factorising

(a) $x^2 + 3x = 28$

(b) $x^2 = 13x - 22$

(c) $x^2 = 19x + 20$

(d) $x^2 = 20 - x$

(e) $x(x + 13) + 36 = 0$

(f) $x(x - 12) = 45$

3 The area of this rectangle is $60\,\text{cm}^2$.

(a) Show that $x^2 + 3x - 88 = 0$

(b) Solve the equation and hence find the dimensions of the rectangle.

 $(x - 4)\,\text{cm}$

$(x + 7)\,\text{cm}$

4 The length of a rectangle is 8 cm more than its width, and its area is $240\,\text{cm}^2$.

(a) By letting the width of the rectangle be x, form an equation in x.

(b) Show that this equation can be simplified to become $x^2 + 8x - 240 = 0$

(c) Solve the equation and hence find the dimensions of the rectangle.

5 Bob's brother is 9 years older than he is. The product of their ages is 90.

(a) By letting b stand for Bob's age, form an equation in b and show that it simplifies to become $b^2 + 9b - 90 = 0$.

(b) Solve this equation to find the ages of the brothers.

6 The triangle and rectangle both have the same area.

(a) Form an equation in x and show that it simplifies to give $x^2 - 9x + 18 = 0$.

(b) Solve the equation and hence find the two possible values for the area.

 $(x - 1)\,\text{cm}$

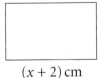

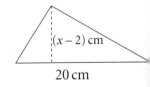 $(x - 2)\,\text{cm}$

$(x + 2)\,\text{cm}$

$20\,\text{cm}$

Section B

1 Expand and simplify

(a) $(2a + 3)(a + 2)$

(b) $(3b + 1)(2b - 3)$

(c) $(p - 5)(4p + 1)$

(d) $(6t - 5)(2t - 1)$

(e) $(r - 9)(2 + 5r)$

(f) $(4x + 1)(4x - 1)$

(g) $(4y + 3)(2 - y)$

(h) $(3t + 1)^2$

(i) $(5 - 2z)^2$

2 Show that the difference in area between the large and small rectangles is $2x^2 + 14x + 5$.

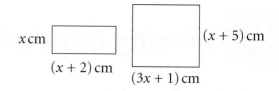

x cm $(x + 5)$ cm

$(x + 2)$ cm $(3x + 1)$ cm

3 Copy and complete

(a) $(2x + 3)($ $) = 2x^2 + 7x + 6$

(b) $($ $)(x - 4) = 2x^2 - 11x + 12$

(c) $(3x - 1)($ $) = 6x^2 + 13x - 5$

(d) $(4x + 3)($ $) = 8x^2 - 6x - 9$

4 Expand and simplify where possible

(a) $(x + 5)(2y + 1)$
(b) $(2x + y)(x - 3y)$
(c) $(5y - 2)(2x + y)$

(d) $(3x - 2y)(x - y)$
(e) $(5x + y)^2$
(f) $(y - 5)(x - 3y)$

(g) $(4x - y)^2$
(h) $(5y - 2x)^2$
(i) $(3x - 2)(5x + 4y)$

Sections C and D

1 Find pairs from the box that multiply to give

(a) $2x^2 + 5x + 2$
(b) $3x^2 + 5x - 2$

(c) $3x^2 - 5x - 2$
(d) $2x^2 - 3x - 2$

> $(3x + 1)$ $(3x - 1)$
> $(x + 2)$ $(x - 2)$
> $(2x + 1)$ $(2x - 1)$

2 Factorise

(a) $2x^2 + 11x + 5$
(b) $3x^2 + 8x + 5$
(c) $3e^2 + 20e - 7$

(d) $7x^2 - 15x + 2$
(e) $5r^2 - 17r + 6$
(f) $2x^2 + 6x - 20$

(g) $3p^2 - 6p + 3$
(h) $4y^2 - 22y + 10$
(i) $35c^2 - 125c - 60$

3 Factorise

(a) $4x^2 + 7x + 3$
(b) $4x^2 + 13x + 3$
(c) $6x^2 - 13x - 5$

(d) $8x^2 + 14x - 15$
(e) $20x^2 - 22x + 6$
(f) $120x^2 + 170x + 60$

4 Factorise

(a) $p^2 - q^2$
(b) $x^2 - 25$
(c) $100y^2 - 1$
(d) $49a^2 - 4b^2$

5 Which three of the following cannot be factorised using integers only?

A $3a^2 + a - 2$
B $3a^2 + a + 2$
C $3a^2 - a - 2$

D $3a^2 - a + 2$
E $2a^2 - a + 3$
F $2a^2 + a - 3$

6 Solve by factorising

(a) $2x^2 - 15x + 7 = 0$
(b) $3x^2 - 5x - 2 = 0$
(c) $2x^2 + 9x + 9 = 0$

(d) $5x^2 - 7x + 2 = 0$
(e) $x^2 - 5x = 0$
(f) $3x^2 + 12x = 0$

(g) $4x^2 + 7x + 3 = 0$
(h) $4x^2 + 28x + 49 = 0$
(i) $2x^2 - 10x + 12 = 0$

(j) $12x^2 + 8x - 15 = 0$
(k) $9x^2 - 24x = 0$
(l) $24x^2 - 40x + 6 = 0$

7 Solve the following quadratic equations by rearranging first.

(a) $2x^2 = x + 10$ (b) $5t^2 + 9t = 6 - 20t$ (c) $6y^2 = 11y - 3$

(d) $12c^2 + 1 = 32c - 20$ (e) $10r = 25 - 8r^2$ (f) $4 - 10a = 10a - 9a^2$

8 Factorise

(a) $10p^2 + 7pq + q^2$ (b) $6r^2 - 7rs - 3s^2$ (c) $8c^2 - 11cd - 10d^2$

Sections E and F

1 Expand and simplify these perfect squares.

(a) $(x + 7)^2$ (b) $(a - 2)^2$ (c) $(c - 8)^2$ (d) $(y + 9)^2$

2 Copy and complete

(a) $(x - \blacksquare)^2 = x^2 - 12x + 36$ (b) $(x + \blacksquare)^2 = x^2 + 30x + 225$

(c) $(x + \blacksquare)^2 = x^2 + 6x + \blacksquare$ (d) $(x - \blacksquare)^2 = x^2 - 18x + \blacksquare$

3 Which of the following expressions are perfect squares?

A $x^2 - 2x + 1$ B $x^2 + 4x - 4$

C $x^2 - x + 1$ D $x^2 - 4x + 4$

4 Solve the following equations. Round to 3 decimal places where necessary.

(a) $(x + 2)^2 = 36$ (b) $(x - 6)^2 = 49$ (c) $(x - 1)^2 = 2$

5 Solve the following equations by using perfect squares, giving each answer correct to 3 decimal places.

(a) $x^2 + 4x - 6 = 0$ (b) $x^2 - 8x - 12 = 0$ (c) $x^2 + 10x + 8 = 0$

(d) $x^2 + 2x - 13 = 0$ (e) $x^2 + 14x + 3 = 0$ (f) $x^2 - 20x + 15 = 0$

6 (a) Expand and simplify $(x + \frac{9}{2})^2$

   (b) Hence solve the equation $x^2 + 9x - 4 = 0$

7 Solve the following equations by using perfect squares, giving each answer correct to 3 decimal places

(a) $x^2 + 5x - 8 = 0$ (b) $x^2 - 7x + 3 = 0$

8 Solve these equations by first dividing, making 1 the coefficient of x^2.

(a) $2x^2 - 10x + 6 = 0$ (b) $4x^2 - 20x - 10 = 0$

(c) $2x^2 + 4x - 3 = 0$ (d) $5x^2 - 5x - 2 = 0$

Section G

1 Use the quadratic formula to solve each equation.

    (a) $x^2 + 3x - 2 = 0$ (b) $x^2 - 6x + 2 = 0$ (c) $2x^2 - 5x + 3 = 0$

    (d) $3x^2 + 4x - 8 = 0$ (e) $5x^2 + 7x + 2 = 0$ (f) $4x^2 - 2x - 7 = 0$

    (g) $2x^2 - 5x = 8$ (h) $9x^2 = 12x + 4$ (i) $8x = x^2 + 5$

2 Solve the following equations, choosing your own method each time.

    (a) $x^2 - 7x + 12 = 0$ (b) $2x^2 + 13x - 7 = 0$ (c) $x^2 + 5x - 14 = 0$

    (d) $x^2 + 8x - 3 = 0$ (e) $3x^2 + 2x - 1 = 0$ (f) $5x^2 - 3x - 4 = 0$

3 (a) Solve the equation $2x^2 + 5x - 3 = 0$

    (b) Hence write down the coordinates of the points where the graph of
        $y = 2x^2 + 5x - 3$ crosses the x-axis.

4 (a) Solve the equations if possible (one of them has no real solutions).

    (i) $x^2 + 4x + 4 = 0$ (ii) $x^2 - 5x + 4 = 0$ (iii) $x^2 + 4x + 5 = 0$ (iv) $x^2 + 5x + 4 = 0$

    (b) Use your solutions to the equations above to help you match each of the following
        equations with one of the graphs.

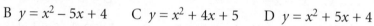

A $y = x^2 + 4x + 4$ B $y = x^2 - 5x + 4$ C $y = x^2 + 4x + 5$ D $y = x^2 + 5x + 4$

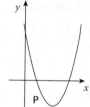
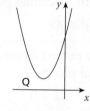

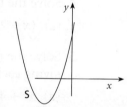

5

    (2x + 3) cm

    Rectangle A   2x cm

    (x − 1) cm

    Rectangle B   (x − 2) cm

The area of rectangle A is 40 cm² greater than the area of rectangle B.

(a) Show that $x^2 + 3x - 14 = 0$

(b) By solving the equation $x^2 + 3x - 14 = 0$, find the value of x correct to 3 d.p.

6 Triangle ABC is right-angled.

The hypotenuse AC is 10 cm longer than the shortest side AB.
The product of these two lengths is 50.

If x cm is the length of AB

(a) Show that $x^2 + 10x - 50 = 0$.

(b) Solve the equation to find the length of the hypotenuse, correct to 2 d.p.

Section H

1 Solve these pairs of simultaneous equations.

   (a) $y = 10x - 16$
         $y = x^2$

   (b) $y = x^2 - 3$
         $y = x + 9$

   (c) $y = 2x^2 + x - 3$
         $y = 2x$

2 Find the points of intersection for each pair of graphs.

   (a)

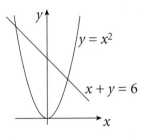

   (b)

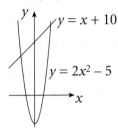

   (c)

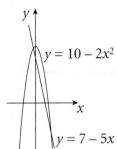

   (d)

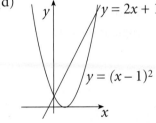

3 Match up the following pairs with the correct description, finding any points of intersection.

A $y = x^2 - 2x$
     $y = 4x - 9$

B $y = 2x^2 + 1$
     $y = 3x - 1$

C $y = 2x^2 - 3x - 1$
     $y = 2x + 2$

The line crosses the curve twice

The line and curve do not intersect

The line just touches the curve

Sections A-G: mixed questions

1 Factorise

   (a) $4x^2 - 6x$ (b) $x^2 - 13x + 36$ (c) $2x^2 + x - 21$

2 Solve the equations

   (a) $x^2 - 2 = 7$ (b) $x^2 - 5x = 0$ (c) $x^2 + 2x = 24$

   (d) $(2x + 1)^2 = 25$ (e) $3x^2 + 16x - 35 = 0$ (f) $x^2 + 7x + 2 = 0$

   (g) $4x^2 + 9x = 0$ (h) $5x^2 - 2x - 4 = 0$

3 The areas of these two rectangles are the same.

   (a) Show that $x^2 + x - 42 = 0$

   (b) Solve this equation and
       hence find the area of each rectangle.

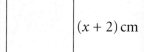
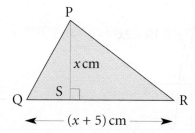

$(x - 3)$ cm $(x + 2)$ cm

$(x + 10)$ cm   6 cm

4 In this diagram, PS = x cm,
QR = $(x + 5)$ cm and angle PSR = 90°.

The area of the triangle is 20 cm².

   (a) Show that $x^2 + 5x - 40 = 0$.

   (b) Solve the equation $x^2 + 5x - 40 = 0$.
       Hence find the length of QR, correct to 2 d.p.

P

x cm

Q   S

R

$(x + 5)$ cm

5 A rectangular pond has a path on four sides as shown.

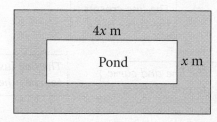

4x m

Pond x m

The pond has dimensions x metres by $4x$ metres.
The path is 2 metres wide.

The total area of the pond and the path is 91 m².

   (a) Show that $4x^2 + 20x - 75 = 0$.

   (b) By solving the equation $4x^2 + 20x - 75 = 0$ find the area of the pond.

6 Angles and circles

Section B

1 Find the angles marked
   with letters.
   Explain how you worked
   out each one.
   O is the centre of each circle.

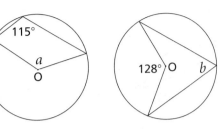 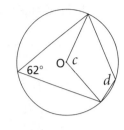

2 C is the centre of the circle.
  Calculate angle ABD, giving a
  reason for each step of working.

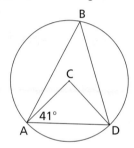

3 C is the centre of the circle.
  Calculate angle ACB, giving a
  reason for each step of working.

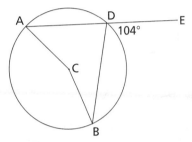

4 Calculate angles BAD and ADC,
  giving reasons for each step
  of working.

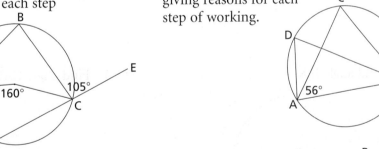

5 Calculate angle ADB
  giving reasons for each
  step of working.

6 C is the centre of the circle.
  Calculate angle EAD, giving a
  reason for each step of working.

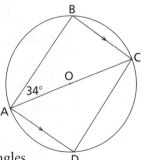

7 In the diagram
  BC is parallel to AD.

(a) Calculate these angles
    (i) ABC (ii) ACB (iii) ADC (iv) CAD
(b) Comment on the line BD
(c) What shape is ABCD?

19

Section C

Give a reason for each step of working in these questions.

1 Find angle ACB

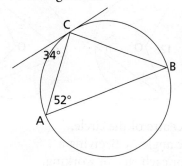

2 Find angle ABC

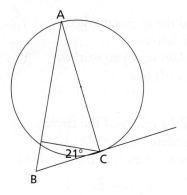

3 Find angle PQS

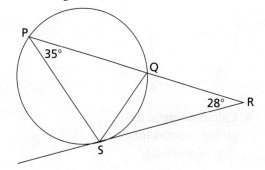

4 Find these angles (a) SPQ (b) SPU

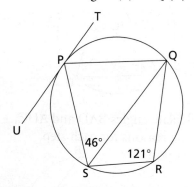

5 Find angle JLK

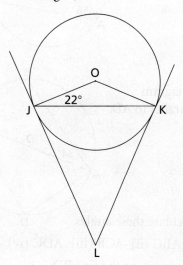

6 Find angle CAD

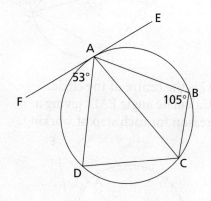

7 Solving inequalities

Section A

1 Copy and complete the following by replacing * with the correct symbol <, >, or =.

    (a) $3 * \pi$ (b) $7 * \sqrt{7}$ (c) $4^2 * 9$ (d) $3 * \sqrt{9}$

2 Match the inequalities with the diagrams

    (a) $n > 3$ (b) $n \le 3$ (c) $3 > n$ (d) $3 \le n$

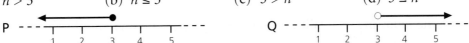

3 Draw number lines to show these inequalities

    (a) $0 < n \le 2$ (b) $^-5 \le n < ^-2$ (c) $4 \le n \le 6$ (d) $6 < n < 12$

4 List all the integers satisfied by these inequalities

    (a) 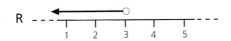   (b) $0 < n < 6$

    (c)    (d) $10 \ge n \ge 6$

    (e) $^-1.2 < n < 0$ (f) $1.8 \le n \le 2.6$

5 Write down the five integers, n, such that $n^2 \le 4$.

6 List all the square numbers, s, such that $0 < s < 20$.

7 List all the factors, f, of 24 such that $1 < f < 8$.

8 (a) If a stands for the size of an angle in degrees, write inequalities
       for each of these statements

       (i) an angle less than 90°

       (ii) an angle between 90° and 180°

       (iii) an angle greater than 180°

    (b) What are the special names given to each of these angles?

9 If l stands for the weight of a letter in grams, write inequalities
   for each of these statements

    (a) letter weighs 60 g or less

    (b) letter weighs more than 60 g up to and including 100 g

    (c) letter weighs over 100 g

Section C

1 Match the inequalities with number line solutions

(a) $x + 3 \geq 7$ (b) $x - 1 < 7$ (c) $\frac{x}{2} \leq 4$ (d) $0 > x - 9$

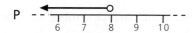

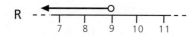
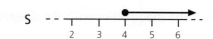

2 Solve the following inequalities and show each solution on a number line

(a) $x + 2 < 1$ (b) $5x \leq 10$ (c) $6 < x - 3$

3 Solve the following inequalities

(a) $3a - 7 < 8$ (b) $6 + 2b \geq 4$ (c) $7 > 2c - 5$

(d) $d - 8 \leq 6$ (e) $9 \leq 12 + 3e$ (f) $\frac{f}{2} + 5 > 7$

(g) $4 + \frac{g}{4} \leq 6$ (h) $3h + 9 > 0$ (i) $0 \leq 1 + \frac{i}{2}$

4 Solve each of these

(a) $3r > r + 7$ (b) $5s \leq s - 8$ (c) $4m + 6 \leq 8m$

(d) $2n - 5 > n$ (e) $4p + 2 \geq 3p$ (f) $2z \leq \frac{z}{2} + 3$

(g) $9l < 4 + l$ (h) $16 + 3q > q$ (i) $\frac{k}{4} + 3 < k$

5 Solve these by first adding the expression in square brackets to both sides

(a) $3 - j > 2$ $[j]$ (b) $8 - 2v \leq 4$ $[2v]$

(c) $9 < 8 - 4t$ $[4t]$ (d) $6 - 2w \geq 3 - 3w$ $[3w]$

6 Solve these inequalities

(a) $3s + 6 > 4s + 1$ (b) $4k - 2 < 5k + 1$ (c) $5f - 8 \geq 3f - 2$

(d) $13 + 2g < 3 + 7g$ (e) $23 - 3h \leq 3 + 7h$ (f) $14 - p > 4 - 2p$

(g) $d + 12 \geq 4 - 3d$ (h) $\frac{w}{3} \geq 14 - 2w$ (i) $7 - \frac{n}{2} \geq 27 - 3n$

7 Multiply out the brackets and then solve the inequalities

(a) $2(x + 2) < 3x + 1$ (b) $2(x + 4) > 3(x + 1)$ (c) $3(2x - 1) \geq 5x$

(d) $3(10 - x) \leq 2(2x + 1)$ (e) $5(3 + x) < 2(4 - x)$ (f) $3(3 + 4x) > 2(x + 7)$

8 First multiply both sides of these inequalities by the number in square brackets and then solve the inequalities.

(a) $\frac{n+2}{4} < n - 4$ $[4]$ (b) $\frac{n-3}{2} \geq 6 - n$ $[2]$ (c) $n - 1 > \frac{n+1}{3}$ $[3]$

(d) $\frac{2n+1}{2} > \frac{4n-1}{3}$ $[6]$ (e) $\frac{5-n}{3} > \frac{6-n}{2}$ $[6]$ (f) $\frac{4-n}{2} \leq \frac{2-5n}{4}$ $[4]$

Section D

1 Which of the two inequalities, A or B, do each of these values of x satisfy?

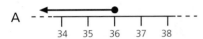 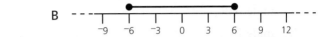

A: $x^2 \leq 4$ B: $x^2 > 4$

  (a) $x = 2$ (b) $x = {}^-1$ (c) $x = 0$

  (d) $x = 3$ (e) $x = {}^-2.6$ (f) $x = {}^-3$

2 Find all the integers such that $x^2 \leq 9$ and $x^2 > 3$.

3 Solve the inequality $x^2 < 36$.
Represent the solution on a number line.

4 Which of these diagrams represents the solution to the inequality $x^2 + 4 \leq 40$?

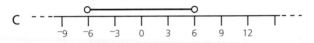

5 Match the inequalities with the number line solutions.

  (a) $x^2 + 8 > 33$ (b) $2x^2 \leq 72$ (c) $3x^2 - 50 < 25$ (d) $7 + 2x^2 \geq 25$

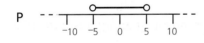 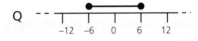

 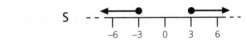

6 Draw a sketch graph of $y = (x + 1)(x - 2)$.
Mark where your graph crosses the x-axis.
Use your graph to write down the solution to $(x + 1)(x - 2) \leq 0$.

7 By sketching graphs or otherwise, solve the inequalities

  (a) $x^2 + 3x + 2 > 0$ (b) $x^2 - 5x + 4 < 0$ (c) $x^2 - 3x - 4 \leq 0$

8 Solve these inequalities and show your solutions on a number line.

  (a) $0 \leq 3x < 15$ (b) $^-3 < 2x + 1 < 3$ (c) $2 < \frac{x}{2} < 4$

9 List all the integers, n, such that

  (a) $2 < 3n - 4 \leq 11$ (b) $1 \leq \frac{n}{2} + 2 < 4$ (c) $^-11 < 4n + 5 \leq 5$

Mixed questions 2

1 Expand and simplify the following.

   (a) $(x + 8)^2$ (b) $(y - 9)^2$ (c) $(a - b)^2$ (d) $(2c - d)^2$

2 A, B, C and D are four points on the
circumference of a circle.
PA is a tangent to the circle at A and
TD is a tangent to the circle at D.
AD is a diameter of the circle.
Angle PAB = 38° and angle TDC = 22°.

Calculate the following angles.
Give reasons for your answers.

   (a) angle ABC

   (b) angle BCD

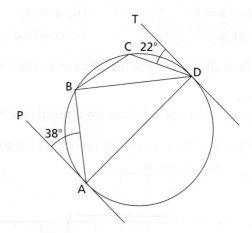

3 (a) Draw a sketch graph of $y = x^2 - x - 12$.
       Mark clearly the values of x where the graph crosses the x-axis.

   (b) Use your graph to write down the solution to $x^2 - x - 12 \geq 0$

4 Mrs Jones invests £250 in a savings account for her grandson at an interest rate of 4% per
annum.

How much is in the account after 10 years?

5 (a) A hanging basket is in the shape of a hemisphere of
       radius 20 cm.

       Calculate the volume of the basket.

   (b) A larger hemispherical hanging basket is made with
       radius 30 cm.

      (i) What is the volume factor for the enlargement?

      (ii) Calculate the volume of the larger basket.

   (c) The number of plants that can grow in the
       hanging basket relates to the surface area of the basket.

       If the smaller basket can hold 8 plants,
       how many can be planted in the larger basket?

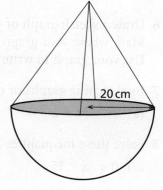

6 Show that the line $y = 1 - x$ does not meet the curve $y = x^2 - 6x + 8$.

7 This table shows the amount spent on electricity each quarter by a household.

Year	1999	2000	2000	2000	2000	2001	2001	2001
Quarter	4	1	2	3	4	1	2	3
Amount	£66	£79	£47	£43	£84	£106	£48	£46

(a) Calculate a 4-point moving average and show it with the original data on a graph.

(b) Describe the trend.

8 Solve the following equations.

(a) $x^2 + 4x + 2 = 0$ (b) $x^2 - 5x - 2 = 0$ (c) $x^2 - 8x + 3 = 0$

9 ABCD is the end wall of a garden store, with dimensions as shown.

(a) Calculate angle ADC.

(b) Calculate the length of the sloping roof CD.

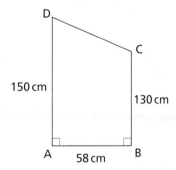

10 The time taken, T hours, for a journey is inversely proportional to the speed of travel, S km/h.

(a) When the speed is 40 km/h, the time taken is 2 hours. The speed is halved to 20 km/h. What is the new time?

(b) Calculate the time when the speed is 64 km/h.

(c) Find an equation expressing T in terms of S.

(d) What is the distance of this journey?

11 (a) Find the prime factorisation of 60 and write it using index notation.

(b) Use prime factorisation to find the LCM of 60 and 48.

(c) Use prime factorisation to find the HCF of 60 and 96.

12 Solve the following inequalities.

(a) $3 - 2x \geq {}^-5$ (b) $3(x - 2) < 4x + 1$ (c) $\frac{x + 2}{3} \leq 4 - x$

13 Anil's dad is 32 years older than Anil is.
In five years time, Anil's dad will be exactly three times as old as Anil.

How old are Anil and his dad now?

8 Trigonometric graphs

Section A

1 Find these to the nearest 0.1° using a calculator.
   Give all the possible answers from ⁻360° to 360°.

   (a) $\sin^{-1} 0.3$ (b) $\sin^{-1} {}^-0.65$ (c) $\sin^{-1} 0.8$

2 What angles between ⁻720° and 720° have the same sine as these?

   (a) 45°   (b) ⁻120°   (c) 610°   (d) ⁻500°

3 Find all possible values of x between 0° and 360° for each of these.

   (a) $3 \sin x = 0.6$ (b) $5 \sin x = 3$ (c) $\frac{1}{2} \sin x = 0.35$ (d) $2 \sin x + 3 = 4$

Section B

1 Find these to the nearest 0.1° using a calculator.
   Give all possible answers from ⁻360° to 360°.

   (a) $\cos^{-1} 0.8$ (b) $\cos^{-1} {}^-0.74$ (c) $\cos^{-1} {}^-0.3$

2 Find all possible values of x between 0° and 360° for each of these.

   (a) $\cos x = 0.2$ (b) $3 \cos x - \frac{1}{4} = 0$

Section C

1 Find all possible values of x between 0° and 360° for each of these.

   (a) $\tan x = 3$ (b) $3 \tan x = {}^-1$ (c) $\cos x = \sin 30$
   (d) $2 \cos x = \tan 60$ (e) $\frac{1}{2} \tan x = \sin 60$ *(f) $\sin 2x = {}^-0.6$

Section D

1 Sketch the following graphs marking on the key points.

   (a) $y = \frac{1}{2} \cos x$ (b) $y = \sin x + 3$ (c) $y = {}^-\sin x$ (d) $y = 2 \cos x - 1$

2 Suggest an equation for each of these graphs.

(a)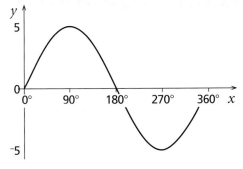

(b)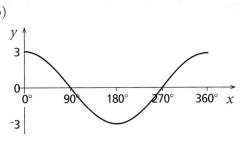

(c)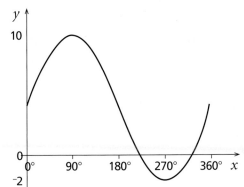

(d)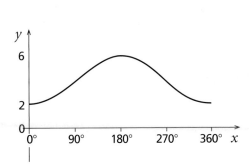

(e)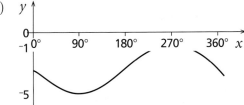

3 Sketch the following graphs marking on the key points.

   (a) $y = \sin(3x)$ (b) $y = 3\cos(2x)$ (c) $y = \sin(4x) + 2$ (d) $y = \cos(\frac{1}{2}x)$

4 Suggest an equation for each of these graphs.

(a)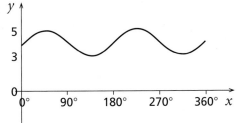

(b)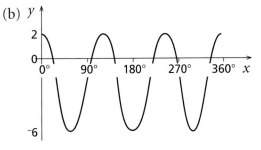

9 Algebraic fractions and equations

Section A

1 Find the value of the following when $x = {}^-1$, $y = \frac{1}{4}$ and $z = 4$.

    (a) x^2y (b) $\dfrac{z}{x}$ (c) $\dfrac{z}{y}$ (d) $\dfrac{x^3}{y^2}$

2 Simplify the following.

    (a) $m^3 \times m^4$ (b) $m^4 \div m^3$ (c) $(m^4)^3$ (d) $(m^3)^4$

3 Simplify the following.

    (a) $\dfrac{4x^2y}{2y}$ (b) $\dfrac{x^2y^3}{xy^2}$ (c) $\dfrac{6a^3b^2}{2a^4b^5}$ (d) $\dfrac{3a^5b^3c^2}{12a^4b^4c^4}$

4 Simplify the following.

    (a) $4x^3 \times 2x^2y^3$ (b) $x^{-3}y^2 \times xy^{-3}$ (c) $(2x^3y)^3$

    (d) $(x^4y^2)^3 \div x^5y^4$ (e) $\sqrt{\dfrac{16x^4y^2}{9p^6q^8}}$

5 Write the following as simply as possible.

    (a) $\dfrac{6a + 9b}{3}$ (b) $\dfrac{3a + 21}{7}$ (c) $\dfrac{6ab - 12b^2}{3b}$

6 Write each of the following as simply as possible as a single fraction.

    (a) $\dfrac{b + 3}{3} - \dfrac{b}{12}$ (b) $\frac{1}{3}(x + 4) + \frac{1}{12}(x - 3)$

    (c) $\dfrac{2a + 3b}{3a} - \dfrac{3a - b}{6a}$ (d) $\dfrac{3ab}{4} \times \dfrac{2a}{b}$

    (e) $\dfrac{4c}{d} \times \dfrac{cd}{2}$ (f) $\dfrac{3p}{2} \div \dfrac{2p}{3}$

    (g) $\dfrac{4a^2bc}{3} \div \dfrac{2ab^2c}{5}$

Sections B and C

1 Simplify and express as a fraction in its simplest form.

(a) $\dfrac{4a+6}{10a+15}$ 　　　　　(b) $\dfrac{x-7}{x^2-5x-14}$ 　　　　　(c) $\dfrac{x-3}{9-3x}$

2 By substituting a value for x show that the following statements **do not** work and explain what has been done incorrectly.

(a) $\dfrac{\not{2}1}{x+\not{2}1}=\dfrac{1}{x+1}$ 　　　　　(b) $\dfrac{\not{x}}{\not{x}+5}=\dfrac{1}{x+5}$

3 Simplify by factorising and then cancelling.

(a) $\dfrac{x^2+x-12}{x-3}$ 　　　　　(b) $\dfrac{5x-25}{x^2-3x-10}$ 　　　　　(c) $\dfrac{x^2-16}{x^2+2x-24}$

4 Copy and complete this simplification.

$$\dfrac{p^2-\blacksquare p-\blacksquare}{p^2-\blacksquare}=\dfrac{p-4}{p-3}$$

5 Write as a single fraction. Simplify your answers where possible.

(a) $\dfrac{3}{4a}+\dfrac{6}{a}$ 　　　　　(b) $\dfrac{3}{x}+\dfrac{x}{5}$ 　　　　　(c) $4-p^{-2}$

6 Write each of these as a single fraction.

(a) $\dfrac{3}{x^2-9}+\dfrac{x}{x+3}$ 　　　　　(b) $2+\dfrac{1}{x^2-1}+\dfrac{x}{x+1}$ 　　　　　(c) $\dfrac{1}{3x+2}-\dfrac{1}{3x-5}$

Sections D and E

1 Solve each of these.

(a) $\dfrac{8}{x}+\dfrac{3x}{x+2}=4$ 　　　　　(b) $\dfrac{3x}{x+1}+\dfrac{x}{x-1}=4$ 　　　　　(c) $\dfrac{x-1}{x+1}=\dfrac{x+2}{x+6}$

2 Solve each of these (you should obtain a quadratic equation to solve).

(a) $\dfrac{3}{x}+4x=13$ 　　　　　(b) $\dfrac{5}{2x+1}+\dfrac{6}{x+1}=3$

(c) $\dfrac{1}{x-1}-\dfrac{1}{x}=8$ 　　　　　(d) $\dfrac{2}{y+1}+\dfrac{3}{2y+3}=1$

3 The sum of the reciprocals of two consecutive numbers is $\dfrac{7}{12}$.
Find the numbers.

4 Rearrange the following to make the letter in the brackets the subject.

(a) $R=\dfrac{st}{m}+\dfrac{sr}{m}$ 　(t) 　　　　　(b) $p=\dfrac{4(q+r)}{q-r}$ 　(q)

(c) $\dfrac{a}{b}+\dfrac{c}{d}=e$ 　(b) 　　　　　(d) $S=\dfrac{y^2}{t}-\dfrac{x^2}{u}$ 　(u)

Section F

1 (a) Simplify this expression $\dfrac{p}{4} + \dfrac{5p}{12} - \dfrac{p}{6}$.

(b) Solve the equation $\dfrac{1}{x-3} - \dfrac{3}{x+2} = \dfrac{1}{2}$.

2 Make p the subject of the formula $r = \sqrt{\dfrac{7}{p-4}}$.

3 Find two consecutive integers whose reciprocals add up to $\dfrac{9}{20}$.

4 Factorise $x^2 + 2x - 255$.

5 Write as a single fraction $\dfrac{5}{x(x+1)} - \dfrac{2}{x^2}$

6 Karl was asked to write $\dfrac{6}{x-2} - \dfrac{4}{x+2}$ as a single fraction in its lowest terms.

Here is his solution.
Find the two mistakes that he made and write out the correct solution.

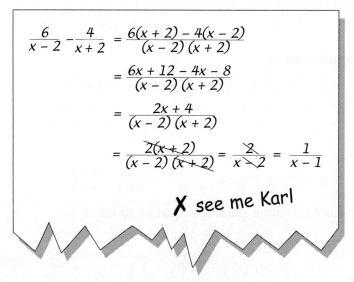

7 Pam is training for a long distance cycle race.
One day she cycles for x hours and travels a distance of 112 km.

(a) Write down, in terms of x, Pam's average speed in km/hr.

The next day she cycles for one hour more to travel the same distance
and her average speed is 2 km/hr slower than the day before.

(b) Show that $x^2 + x - 56 = 0$.

(c) Calculate the number of hours Pam cycles on the second day.

10 Pattern and proof

Sections A, B and C

1 Copy and complete the first five terms of these linear sequences.

    (a) 4, 10, _____ , 22 , _____   (b) 42, _____ , 34 , _____ , 26

    (c) $p, p + 3,$ _____ , _____, _____   (d) $s - 4,$ ____ , $s + 6$, $s + 11,$ ___

2 These are the first four terms of a linear sequence.

    5, 9, 13, 17

    (a) What are the next two terms of the sequence?

    (b) Find an expression for the nth term of the sequence.

    (c) What is the 20th term of the sequence?

    (d) Show that 120 cannot be a term in this sequence.

    (e) Which term in this sequence is 105?

3 Match the expressions for the nth term to the correct sequence.

    A $n^2 + n - 3$ B $n^2 + n - 1$ C $3n^2 + 2n - 6$

    D $2n^2 + 3n - 4$ E $2n^2 - 3n$ F $4n - 3$

    (a) 1, 5, 9, 13   (b) 1, 5, 11, 19   (c) ⁻1, 10, 27, 50

    (d) ⁻1, 3, 9, 17   (e) ⁻1, 2, 9, 20   (f) 1, 10, 23, 40

4 A quadratic sequence begins 5, 9, 15, 23, ...

    (a) Find the next two terms of this sequence.

    (b) Find an expression for the nth term of this sequence.

    (c) Show that 423 is the 20th term in this sequence.

5 Write down the first three terms of the sequence where the nth term is:

    (a) $4n + 3$ (b) $n^4 + 2$ (c) $2n + 4$

    (d) $\dfrac{24}{n}$ (e) $\dfrac{n}{n + 3}$ (f) $n^3 - n^2$

6 Give the nth term of the following sequences

    (a) 0, 3, 8, 15, 24, ...

    (b) 2, 6, 12, 20, 30, ...

    (c) 2, 6, 10, 14, 18 ....

    (d) 1, 8, 27, 64, 125

    (e) $\dfrac{2}{3}, \dfrac{3}{7}, \dfrac{4}{11}, \dfrac{5}{15}, \dots$

    (f) 20, 17, 14, 11, 8 ....

    (g) 2, 7, 14, 23, 34 ...

Section D

1 Show that each of these statements is false.

    A $2n + 1$ is odd for all values of n.

    B $24n > 24$ for all values of n.

2 State which one of these statements is false.
Use a counterexample to show that it is false.

    A $n^2 + 3n > {}^-2$ for all positive values of n.

    B $n^2 + 4n + 6$ is even for all values of n.

    C $n^2 - 2n > 15$ for all values of n greater then 5.

Section E and F

1 Each of these walls is made with cubes.

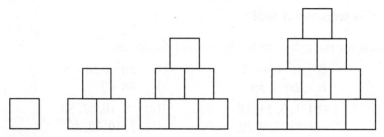

    (a) Find an expression for the number of cubes in the nth model.

    (b) How many cubes are in the 10th wall?

2 Prove that the product of two positive numbers is always less than the square of the sum of them.

3 Prove that the sum of the squares of two consecutive numbers is always odd.

4 (a) Write expressions for four consecutive numbers, where the smallest is p.

    (b) Prove that the sum of the four consecutive numbers is equal
to the difference between the product of the last pair
and the product of the first pair.

5 (a) You can place a three by three square anywhere on this grid.

1	2	3	4	5	6	7	8
9	10	11	12	13	14	15	16
17	18	19	20	21	22	23	24
25	26	27	28	29	30	31	32
33	34	35	36	37	38	39	40
41	42	43	44	45	46	47	48
49	50	51	52	53	54	55	56
57	58	59	60	61	62	63	64
65	66	67	68	69	70	71	72

(i) If the lowest number in the square is k, write an expression for each of the corner numbers in the square.

(ii) Prove that the difference between the products of the opposite corners of the square is always 32.

*(b) Prove that the difference of the opposite corner products for any size square placed on this grid will be a multiple of 8.

*6 All prime numbers greater than 3 can be written in the form $6n + 1$ or $6n - 1$.

Prove that the difference of the squares of any two prime numbers greater than 3 is a multiple of 12.

11 Histograms

Section A

1 This histogram shows the distribution of the lengths of a group of babies.

Copy and complete this frequency table:

Length, l cm	Frequency
$60 < l \le 64$	
$64 < l \le 66$	
$66 < l \le 68$	
$68 < l \le 70$	
$70 < l \le 74$	

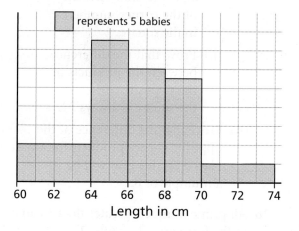

represents 5 babies

Length in cm

2 A company surveyed its employees to find out the distance they each travelled to work.

The results are summarised in the table below.

Distance, d km	Frequency
$0 < d \le 5$	10
$5 < d \le 10$	22
$10 < d \le 20$	15
$20 < d \le 50$	6
$50 < d$	0

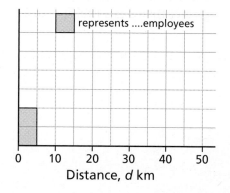

represents ....employees

Distance, d km

The bar for $0 < d \le 5$ has been drawn.

(a) What does one square on the histogram represent?

(b) Copy and complete the histogram.

Sections B and C

1 A survey was carried out to find out the amount of pocket money received each week by a group of secondary school pupils.

The distribution is shown in this histogram.

(a) How many pupils received less than £4 each week?

(b) How many pupils received more than £8 each week?

(c) How many pupils were surveyed altogether?

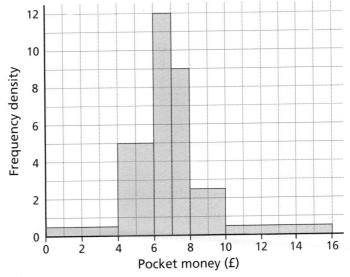

2 Copy and complete the frequency table below, using the information in the histogram.

Weight, w g	Frequency
$20 < w \leq 40$	
$40 < w \leq 50$	
$50 < w \leq 60$	
$60 < w \leq 80$	

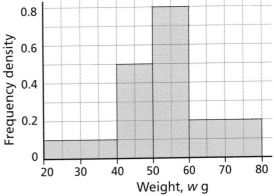

3 This table shows the distribution of weights of a group of 15-year-old boys.

Weight, w kg	Frequency
$30 < w \leq 40$	2
$40 < w \leq 50$	10
$50 < w \leq 55$	15
$55 < w \leq 60$	13
$60 < w \leq 70$	6
$70 < w \leq 90$	4

(a) Calculate the frequency density for each interval.

(b) Draw a histogram for the data.

35

4 The unfinished histogram and table give information about the length of time taken by some members of a health club to run one mile.

Use the information to copy and complete the table and histogram.

Time, t minutes	Frequency
$5 < t \leq 8$	
$8 < t \leq 9$	
$9 < t \leq 10$	13
$10 < t \leq 12$	8
$12 < t \leq 14$	2

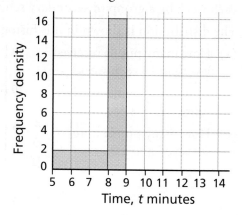

5 This table shows the distribution of ages of cars parked in a car park.

Draw a histogram for the data.

Age, A years	Frequency
$0 < A \leq 1$	6
$1 < A \leq 3$	27
$3 < A \leq 6$	15
$6 < A \leq 10$	14
$10 < A \leq 20$	3

Mixed questions 3

1 Find all the possible values of x between $0°$ and $360°$ for each of these.

  (a) $\sin 2x = 0.5$ (b) $\cos\left(\frac{x}{2}\right) = {}^-0.2$ (c) $\tan 3x = 2$ (d) $5\cos 2x = {}^-3$

2 Write down the first five terms of the sequences that have the following nth terms.

  (a) $4n - 3$ (b) $2 - 3n^2$ (c) $n^3 + 2n^2 - 1$ (d) $\frac{3}{n}$

3 Hayley trains regularly at a health club.
  She runs on the treadmill for $4\,\text{km}$ at $x\,\text{km/h}$ then she cycles for $3\,\text{km}$ at $(x - 5)\,\text{km/h}$.

  (a) Hayley exercises for exactly 1 hour.
     Form an equation in x and show that it simplifies to $x^2 - 12x + 20 = 0$

  (b) Solve this equation and find the speeds at which Hayley runs and cycles.

4 A group of students were surveyed to find out the
number of text messages they sent in a week.

The distribution is shown in this histogram.

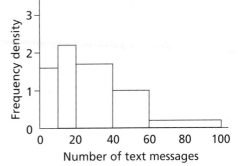

  (a) How many students sent
     less than 10 text messages?

  (b) How many students sent
     more than 40 text messages?

  (c) How many students were
     surveyed altogether?

  (d) Estimate the number of students
     who sent between 30 and 40 texts in a week.

5 Solve

  (a) $x + 5 \geq \frac{x+2}{4}$ (b) $\frac{x-3}{2} \leq \frac{x}{5}$ (c) $\frac{x+1}{x+2} > \frac{x+1}{x-2}$

6 This is a sketch of the graph $y = \cos x$.

  Sketch the following graphs

  (a) $y = 3\cos x$

  (b) $y = {}^-\cos(3x)$

  (c) $y = \cos x + 3$

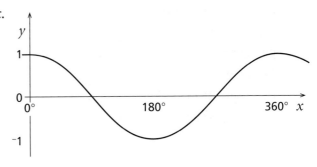

7 Prove that the sum of any six consecutive numbers is a multiple of three.

8 (a) The graph of the formula $x^2 + y^2 = a^2$ is a circle.
Rearrange this formula to make y the subject.

(b) The graph of the formula $\dfrac{x^2}{a^2} - \dfrac{y^2}{b^2} = 1$ is a curve called a hyperbola.
Rearrange this formula to make y the subject.

9 One light year is about 9.4×10^{12} km.
Alpha Centauri is the closest star to Earth. It is 4.34 light years from Earth.

How many kilometres is it from Alpha Centauri to Earth?

10 A line has equation $y = 4x - 3$.

(a) What is the gradient of the line?

(b) What are the coordinates of the y-intercept?

(c) Find the equation of the line perpendicular to the line $y = 4x - 3$, which passes through the point $(0, 4)$.

11 The price of a washing machine is reduced by 15% in a sale.
The reduced price is £331.50.

(a) Calculate the original price of the washing machine.

(b) The shop offers 6 months interest free credit on all sale goods.
They ask for a deposit of 20% of the sale price and then six equal paymentsof the remainder.

Calculate the deposit and monthly payments for the washing machine.

12 Solve these pairs of simultaneous equations.

(a) $4x + y = 18$
$3x + 2y = 7$

(b) $y = x^2 - 2$
$y = 2x + 1$

13 A, B, C and D are points on the circumference of a circle.
O is the centre of the circle.

Calculate these angles,
giving reasons for each step of your working.

(a) angle ABC

(b) angle BCO

(c) angle ADC

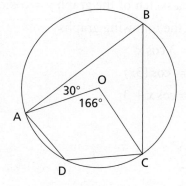

14 Make T_1 the subject of the formula $W = \dfrac{R}{1-n}\,(T_2 - T_1)$.

15 This vase is a frustum of a cone.

Calculate its volume.

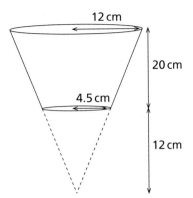

12 cm

20 cm

4.5 cm

12 cm

16 This table shows the distribution of weights of a group of babies at their 6-month health check.

(a) Make a cumulative frequency table.

(b) Draw a cumulative frequency graph of the distribution.

(c) Estimate

    (i) their median weight

    (ii) the lower quartile

    (iii) the upper quartile

    (iv) the interquartile range

Weight (w, kg)	Frequency
6.0 < w 6.5	8
6.5 < w 7.0	10
7.0 < w 7.5	24
7.5 < w 8.0	35
8.0 < w 8.5	33
8.5 < w 9.0	21
9.0 < w 9.5	15
9.5 < w 10.0	4

17 Write as a single fraction

(a) $\dfrac{r+1}{2} + \dfrac{2r-1}{3r}$ (b) $\dfrac{b}{3} - \dfrac{4-3b}{2}$ (c) $\dfrac{4e^2}{5} \times \dfrac{3}{2e}$ (d) $\dfrac{4s^2t}{3} \div \dfrac{6s^2t}{t}$

18 (a) Work out how many matchsticks would be needed for each of the first five of these patterns

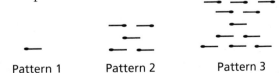

Pattern 1   Pattern 2   Pattern 3

(b) Find a rule for the number of matchsticks in the nth pattern.

(c) One of these matchstick patterns can be made using 419 matchsticks. Which pattern is it?